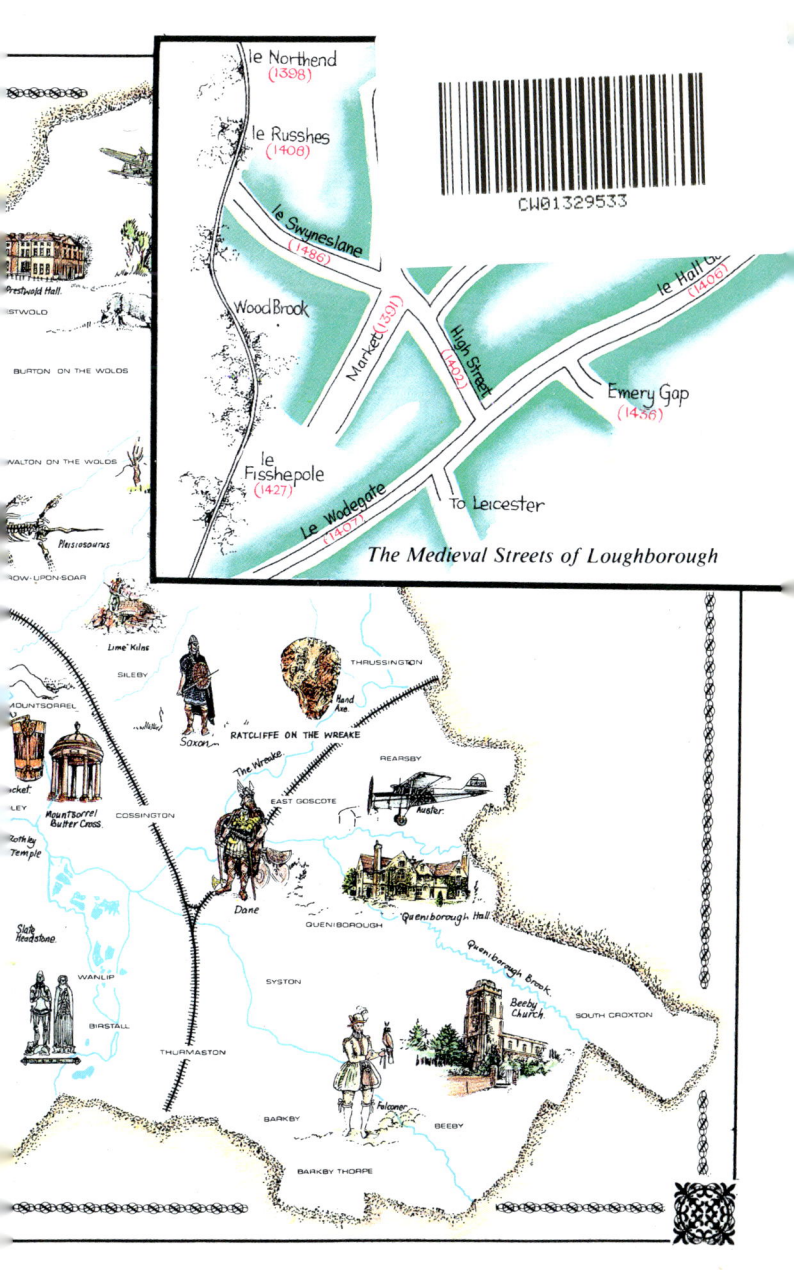

The Medieval Streets of Loughborough

- le Northend (1398)
- le Russhes (1408)
- le Swyneslane (1486)
- Wood Brook
- Market (1501)
- High Street (1402)
- le Hall Ga... (1406)
- Emery Gap (1436)
- le Fisshepole (1427)
- Le Wodegate (1407)
- To Leicester

Prestwold Hall
BURTON ON THE WOLDS
WALTON ON THE WOLDS
Plesiosaurus
ROW-UPON-SOAR

Lime Kilns
SILEBY
Saxon
THRUSSINGTON
Hand Axe
RATCLIFFE ON THE WREAKE
MOUNTSORREL
Mountsorrel Butter Cross
...th by Temple
The Wreake
COSSINGTON
Dane
REARSBY
Auster
EAST GOSCOTE
Queniborough Hall
QUENIBOROUGH
Queniborough Brook
Slate Headstone
WANLIP
BIRSTALL
SYSTON
Beeby Church
SOUTH CROXTON
THURMASTON
Falconer
BARKBY
BEEBY
BARKBY THORPE

University Town of LOUGHBOROUGH
Twinned with Epinal, France and Schwäbisch Hall, Germany

In the Domesday Book of 1086, Loughborough's name was given as Lucteburne. *Lucte* was probably a man's name, and *burne* a mistake by the scribe; it should have been *burg*. The whole word means 'Luhhede's defended place'; there may have been a stockade around the town in its very early days.

Acknowledgments
　The authors and publishers wish to thank the following for their help in the preparation of this book: A R C Ltd; Borough of Charnwood – Messrs K Carson, D Harris, B Henman and W D Maltby; William Davis (Leicester) Ltd; Mrs Gilby, Dishley Grange Farm; Hawker Siddeley plc – Messrs A Jarrom, B Hope and G Toms; Mr D Jones; Mrs Merriman; Mr W Moffatt; Mr R Playfair; Stahl Chemicals (GB) Ltd; John Storer House; John Taylor's Bell Foundry – Mr A P S Berry and Mr T S Jennings; 3M Health Care Ltd; Mr T M Walters.
　Illustrations on front endpapers and pages 8/9, 12, 13, 14, 18 (top), 19 and 20 by Ray Weston.
　Photographs by courtesy of: B & H (Leicester) Ltd – page 41 (bottom); British Library – page 7 (top); British Waterways Museum – page 21 (bottom left); Butterley Bricks Ltd – page 19 (top); Central Television – page 23 (bottom); Tim Clark – biblio and title page photographs, also pages 5, 9 (top), 11, 13 (centre), 16 (top), 19 (centre and bottom), 21 (2), 24, 25 (top), 27 (bottom), 35 (left), back endpaper (top right); Fisons plc – pages 40 (bottom), 41 (top); Great Central Railway – page 22 (centre and bottom); Hawker Siddeley plc – pages 31 (top and bottom), 33 (2); Hunting Aerofilms – page 42 (bottom); Mr John Knighton – back endpaper (left); Ladybird Books Ltd – pages 36, 37; Leicestershire Museums, Art Galleries and Record Services – page 19 (bottom), 26 (top); *Loughborough and Coalville Trader* – back endpaper (bottom right); Loughborough Library Collection – pages 9 (bottom), 13 (top), 15 (top), 17 (bottom), 25 (bottom), 28, 29, 30 (top), 32 (bottom), 40 (centre); Loughborough University A V S – pages 15 (bottom), 42 (top), 43 (top); Davy Morris Ltd – pages 38, 39; Dr Marilyn Palmer – page 16 (bottom); Mr Mark Pearson – page 23 (top); Paul Popper Ltd – page 17 (top); Mr Jeff Taylor – page 32 (top); John Taylor's Bell Foundry – pages 34 (2), 35 (right); Towles plc – page 30 (bottom left and right); University of Exeter – page 7 (bottom); R Vittols, G Ward and G Wray – page 43 (bottom). Cover photographs by Tim Clark; map by Ordnance Survey (Crown copyright reserved).
　Book and cover designed by R W Ditchfield.

British Library Cataloguing in Publication Data
Wix, Don
　Loughborough past and present
　1. Leicestershire. Loughborough
　I. Title　II. Humphrey, Wallace　　III. Keil, Ian　　IV. Series
　942.5'47
　ISBN 0-7214-1125-8

First edition

Published by Ladybird Books Ltd Loughborough Leicestershire UK
Ladybird Books Inc Auburn Maine 04210 USA

© LADYBIRD BOOKS LTD MCMLXXXVIII
All rights reserved. No part of this publication may be reproduced, stored in a retrieval system, or transmitted in any form or by any means, electronic, mechanical, photo-copying, recording or otherwise, without the prior consent of the copyright owner.

Printed in England

Loughborough
Past and Present

by DON WIX, WALLACE HUMPHREY
and IAN KEIL

Ladybird Books

The Borough Arms

In the days when knights wore armour, it was difficult to tell one from another, so they had designs painted on their shields.

A complete collection of such designs was known as an *achievement*, and it included: a shield (sometimes called a coat of arms because it was often shown on a surcoat, or mantle, worn over the armour to protect it from rain, and to shade the man from the sun); a crest; and a motto. Experts known as heralds were trained to identify fighting men by designs of this kind.

As time went by, towns, and groups of people in the same trade, could apply for arms. Loughborough did so when it became a borough in 1888, and the designs were based on those of three important families who had once owned the town, the Despensers, the Beaumonts and the Hastings.

Here are some special names which heralds use for each different part of a design.

Gold is OR.

Black is SABLE.

A bar is a BEND.

Cockleshells are ESCALLOPS.

A lion with only one paw on the ground is RAMPANT.

A lace pattern is a FRET.

A lady's sleeve, given by her as a favour to her knight, is a MAUNCH.

The Mayor and Macebearer in official dress

The bull's head is ERASED (torn off with ragged edges).

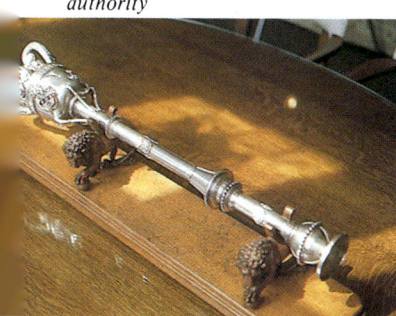

The Mace is a symbol of the Mayor's authority

Loughborough and the Domesday Book

Loughborough's entry in the Domesday Book

In William the Conqueror's Domesday Book of 1086 Loughborough farmed nineteen carucates, which was about 2280 acres. (When it was measured in 1762, about seven hundred years later, it was almost the same – 2142 acres.)

Next in importance to the land was the machinery to cultivate the soil. The lord had five ploughs for his land and the villagers twelve and a half for theirs. Half a plough seems a strange idea but the word in this instance included the oxen needed to pull it.

Ploughing with oxen

Sowing seed by hand

Only forty four people are mentioned in the Domesday Book, but they were men with families, so the population was probably about 176. (Today it is about 52,000.) About one third had Danish ancestors: they were more important than the English because they had more rights.

Everyone farmed for a living, but on the river Soar there were two watermills where the corn was ground into flour. Near the Soar, there were also forty five acres of meadow.

There was some woodland, seven furlongs long and three furlongs wide, probably the area now called the Outwoods.

At this time, there was no real freedom. The villagers could not leave, and their daughters could not marry without the lord's permission. Farming had to be done to a set plan, decided before ploughing time.

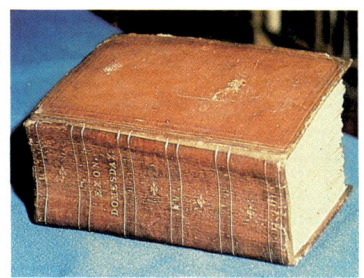

A bound copy of the Domesday Book

Mills

Over one thousand years ago people were keen to use machinery where they could. In 1086 there were two watermills on the river Soar at Cotes, and two on the Black Brook, at Dishley and Garendon.

Mills were so important all over the country that lords of the manor, to whom they belonged, made it compulsory for local people to use them. In the sixteenth century, however, the owners of the mills at Dishley and Garendon (not then in Loughborough) cut their charges to draw people away from the two mills at Cotes. Later on, competition increased when Quorn watermill and Knight Thorpe windmill also offered cheap terms.

A windmill in 18th century Loughborough

Inside an old watermill

Between 1610 and 1697 the lords of the manor of Loughborough asked the law courts, time after time, to pass laws to make Loughborough people use their mills. For a long time people had to give way but in 1697, after a bitter struggle, they won their right to take their corn where they wished.

The lower mill still stands at Cotes today. The upper mill was about 800 yards away but had to be destroyed, because it caused flooding.

Cotes Mill today

Dishley Mill on the Black Brook in the 19th century

The Manor of Loughborough

A manor was land given by the king to be used by one of his supporters. The first lord of the manor of Loughborough after 1066 was the Earl of Chester. Next were the Despensers, two of whom were hanged for rebellion. They were followed by the Beaumonts – until one of them became insane. Next came the Greys of Bradgate, and both Lady Jane and her father were executed.

The Hastings were the last of the powerful lords of the manor. They steadily sold their land however and after 1818 the only important privilege remaining to them was the control of Loughborough Market.

A manor house had been built in 1477; at least one wall of this and an open fireplace as well are now part of the Burdell Restaurant in Sparrow Hill. It was sold by the

A stained glass window showing Lord Hastings

10

Hastings family in 1654. Part of Lowe's furniture shop is perhaps as old as the Manor House, and is shown below.

The Manor House today

Another old building is the Rectory, the oldest parts having been built around 1300. These three buildings and the Church of All Saints were in the oldest area of the original town.

The remains of the old Rectory

11

Market Place

The Market Place started as a meeting area on open land west of the main London to Manchester road. Church Gate, Baxter Gate and Biggin Street appear in documents at about the same time. Later there appear High Gate, Hall Gate and Woodgate, leading to the Outwoods.

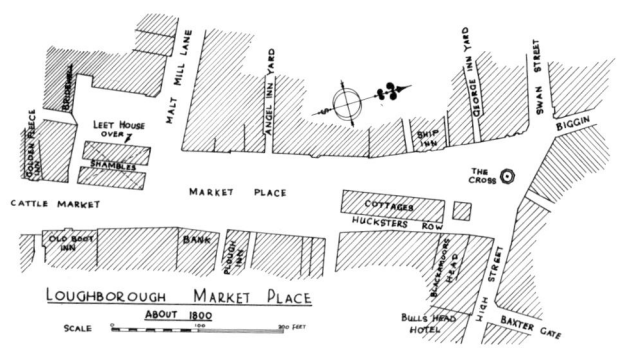

In 1221 King Henry III granted permission for Loughborough to hold a market every Thursday and a two-day fair yearly on 1st August.

After six years, in 1227, the fair was extended to three days and was later moved to mid November. As Loughborough grew in importance as a market town, folks from surrounding villages visited the Butter and Hen Cross to buy and sell their country wares. Weekly market traders have always paid a toll for their stalls, originally based on the amounts of fruit, vegetables, poultry, fish and animals brought for sale.

Butter and Hen Cross

Wrongdoers were punished in the stocks or at the whipping post which were both removed about 1820

Today, as through the ages, the busy Market Place reflects a prosperous town.

The Market Place in the 1870s

The Fair

These days fair and fun go together. When King Henry III granted a charter to Loughborough permitting the holding of a fair, however, the value was then in the variety of the business that took place. The fair was held once a year, on St Peter's Day to start with. The lord of the manor organised it, and received fees from stallholders. He made sure that deals were enforced with justice at a special court of law where wrongdoers were fined.

Many people went to the fair to buy goods not usually available elsewhere. A great variety of things were sold – luxuries like jewellery, cloth imported from abroad such as silk, and unusual foods and drinks.

A jester

Traders bought special tools or materials for their work. Some people came to have painful teeth removed or to buy medicines for illnesses. Hiring workers for the year was another activity. Men and women with skills to offer came to the fair to meet employers and they then agreed about wages for a year. Until the middle

A street entertainer

of the nineteenth century the fair had all these serious purposes. Then other ways of doing business gradually took away all but pleasure.

Over the years entertainment has changed. Engineering developments have brought high speed rides, loud music and bright lights.

Early 20th century roundabout

The fair today

Battles and Riots

About one thousand years ago there was a great deal of fighting in Leicestershire. The Danes conquered the county in 877, and later the Norwegians did a lot of damage between 940 and 942. William the Conqueror may also have laid waste to part of Leicestershire because it was held by an enemy nobleman, Earl Eadwine.

In 1644 there was a local battle in the Civil War between King and Parliament. It was fought between Royalists who wanted to cross Cotes Bridge to get to Newark, and Parliamentary soldiers who were sent to stop them.

Cotes Bridge

King Charles I himself stayed overnight at Cotes Hall in 1645, when he and his army were on the way to capture Leicester.

Re-enactment of the battle at Cotes Bridge

In 1816 there was another kind of battle between John Heathcoat, the lace manufacturer, and a group of men called Luddites, who were against the idea of any new machinery which might make people lose their jobs. They did much damage at Heathcoat's factory.

A Zeppelin

On 31st January 1916, during the First World War, Loughborough was attacked by a Zeppelin (a German airship). Four bombs were dropped and ten people were killed. Eight years later an unexploded aerial torpedo was found in the canal.

Bomb-damaged houses in The Rushes in 1916

Plague

In Loughborough between 1348 and 1390 there were five outbreaks of the Black Death. It was given this name because the disease caused bleeding under the skin, turning it a dark colour. As many as one person in every three may have died because of the Black Death.

In 1558 the Great Plague began in Loughborough and lasted on and off for more than a century. Its victims died in agony, with fever and painful swelling in parts of their bodies. We know how many people were thought to have died from it because the letter 'p' was written in the Parish Register against the name of each victim.

Doctors were protected by plague masks

In 1848 there was an outbreak of cholera, caused by dirty water. Loughborough was not the healthy place it is today – one child in every five died before its first birthday.

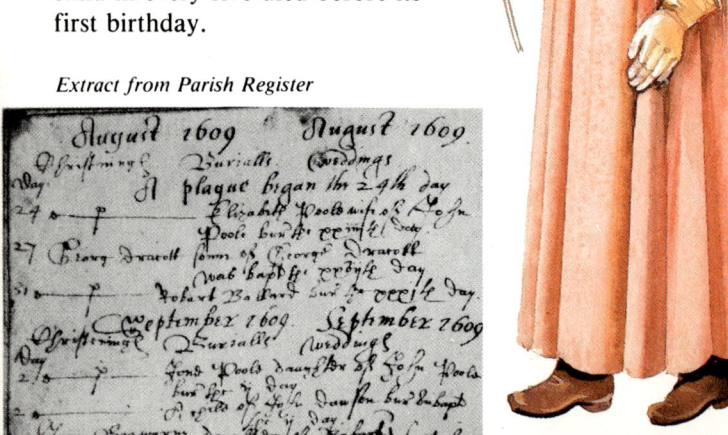

Extract from Parish Register

Local Rocks

Loughborough's buildings make use of many different kinds of rocks that are to be found in the surrounding area.

Slate 55,000,000 years old

Swithland slate quarry (disused)

Sand and gravel
100,000 years old

William Davis's sand and gravel workings at Wanlip

Red clay
200,000,000 years old

Tucker's Brickworks up to 1965

Granite
700,000,000 years old

A.R.C.'s Longcliffe granite quarry

Coal
250,000,000 years old

Snibston colliery

Cross section of local rocks

MINING VILLAGES — CHARNWOOD HEIGHTS — SWITHLAND — TOWN TERRACE — FLOOD PLAIN — WOLDS

SEAMS — PRE-CAMBRIAN ROCKS (GRANITE TYPE) — SLATE — GRAVEL — SILT — RED CLAY

Waterways

As soon as coal began to be mined in large quantities, inland waterways were developed to carry the heavy loads.

There were two kinds. One was the navigation, where a river was used, with cuts between sections that were too shallow. For example, there is a cut at Zouch. The other kind of waterway was the canal, which was completely manmade.

In Leicestershire the earliest waterway was the Loughborough Navigation, opened in 1778. It connected the town with the river Trent. Another waterway led to the Derbyshire coalfield. Narrow boats carried heavy loads of all kinds and came to a stop at Bridge Street. A brewery, gas and electricity works were built next to The Rushes, because the coal was delivered nearby.

Early 19th century canal map

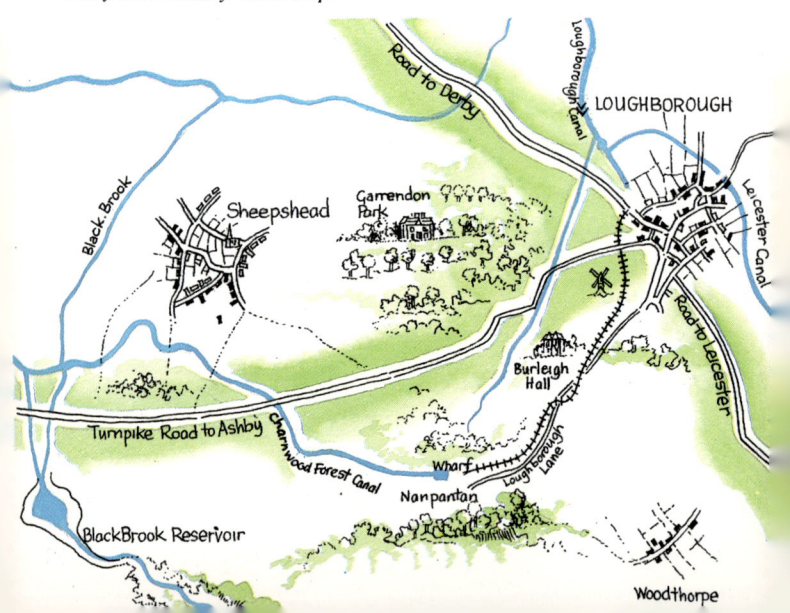

The bed of the old Charnwood Canal at Nanpantan

By 1836, 3400 tons of Derbyshire coal were passing along the navigations weekly.

To give Leicestershire mines a chance to sell their coal, the Charnwood Forest Canal had been opened in 1796. It ran from Thringstone to Nanpantan, but was expensive to run and gradually fell into disuse.

In 1840 however a railway was built between Derby and Leicester. Since it carried heavy goods more cheaply and more quickly than the navigations, they slowly declined. Today they are used by pleasure craft.

Canal art decoration

The Grand Union Canal today

Railways

The first railways in the county were those at either end of the Charnwood Forest Canal, used for horse-drawn loads. The second was one between Swannington and Leicester, which used steam locomotives and was completed in 1833. The third was the Midland Counties Railway, which ran from Derby and Nottingham, the two lines meeting near the river Trent and going on through Loughborough and Leicester to Rugby. From there travellers could get to London.

No. 506 Butler-Henderson *leaving Loughborough*

The steamtrain Mayflower *with the diesel electric* Atlantic Conveyor *in the Great Central sheds*

Thomas Cook's first excursion from Leicester to Loughborough on 5th July 1841

The first train carrying passengers from Leicester passed through Loughborough at eight o'clock on the morning of 5th May 1840, and nearly everybody in the town turned out to see it. The cheapest fare for this journey was 1s. 6d. (7½ pence).

Another line, the Charnwood Forest Railway, was built from near Coalville to Loughborough (Derby Road) in 1883. This was closed to passengers in 1931. The Station Hotel still stands on Derby Road; it was built opposite the end of the line.

The last railway was the Great Central, opened in 1899. It was hoped that it would eventually reach France, through a Channel tunnel, but it was closed by British Rail in 1967.

A TV series on location at Great Central Station – Shine On, Harvey Moon

Water and Drainage

After the outbreak of cholera in 1848 a Local Board of Health was set up to improve matters.

It took the town over forty years to build the sewage disposal works at Swingbridge Lane. It was only then that the problems were solved.

Nanpantan Reservoir

To provide a good supply of pure water, a reservoir was opened at Nanpantan in 1870. To celebrate this event, a fountain was erected in the Market Place by Archdeacon Fearon, of All Saints Church. He had been trying for over twenty years to persuade people that the reservoir was needed.

Archdeacon Fearon

Nanpantan water was not enough, however, for the expanding town, and another reservoir using the Blackbrook was opened in 1906.

The Fountain, Market Place

Now the town's water is supplied by the Severn-Trent Water Authority, mainly from the rivers Dove and Derwent, in Derbyshire.

Blackbrook Dam under construction, early 1900s

Robert Bakewell – Agricultural Pioneer

Born in 1725, Robert Bakewell was farming 400 acres at Dishley by 1760, and was widely known for good farm management. He was a well travelled man full of new ideas – ideas that were to change farming in Britain.

In his time fields were being enclosed by fences and hedges, and almost the whole of Leicestershire then became good land for grazing. Bakewell was a stockbreeder, and he produced the Dishley Longhorn. His famous bull, Twopenny, lived for twenty six years.

Robert Bakewell

Dishley Longhorn bull

The New Leicester sheep, at first called the Dishley breed, was another of his successes. The need for more meat in Britain led Bakewell to breed a new shape of sheep with 'clean heads; straight, broad, flat backs and round barrel-like bodies.' His aim was 'to produce 2 lbs of mutton where there was only 1 lb before.'

New Leicester sheep

Local farmers visited Dishley Farm to improve their own flocks of sheep with Bakewell's stock at a £105 fee – a very large fee for the time.

Dishley Grange today

Lace and Hosiery

Although engineering was growing in importance when Loughborough became a borough in 1888, much of the work of the town was in hosiery manufacture. By that time many factories had been built.

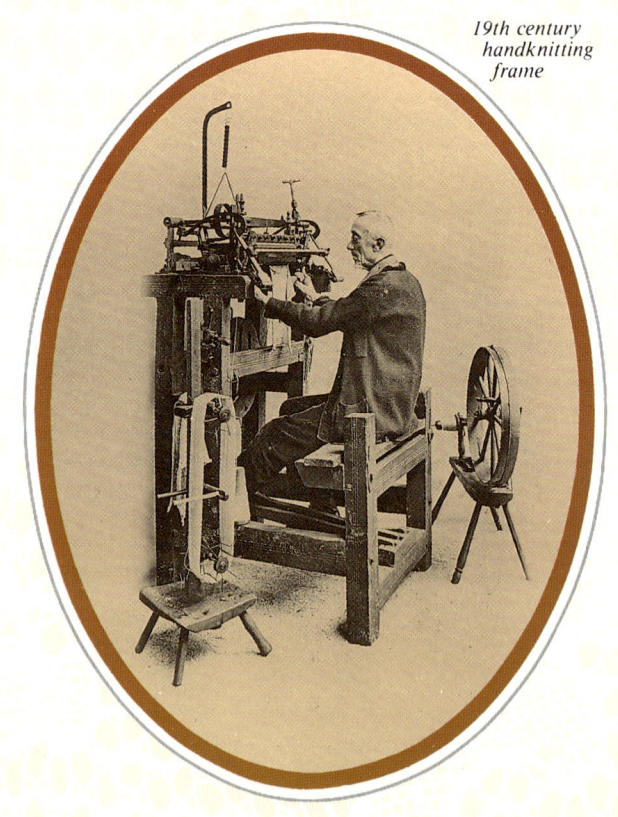

19th century handknitting frame

Stockings and other clothes had once been made in the homes of the workers. They used a 'knitting frame' invented about two hundred years earlier.

People often spent fifteen hours a day bending over the garments they were making. Everybody found something to do, even children about five years old. Mothers and older children finished off work knitted on the frame by fathers, so there was little time for cooking or cleaning the house.

People did not want to work new machinery, and it seemed that nothing was ever likely to change in hosiery.

In 1809 another trade had come to Loughborough. John Heathcoat invented the world's first lace making machine and opened a factory in the town. His men were well paid and people flooded in to work as 'lace hands'. There were 4546 people in the town in 1801; by 1821 the population was 7365.

Cartwright and Warner's early hosiery factory by the canal

In Loughborough people went on making lace and the population went on growing. In 1831 it was 10,800. But gradually the trade moved to the Nottingham area and as late as 1861 Loughborough had only 10,830 people.

Then in 1864 William Cotton invented a machine to do automatically most of what the old knitting frames had done in the hosiery industry. These new machines were put into factories; the town grew and workers earned better wages.

William Cotton

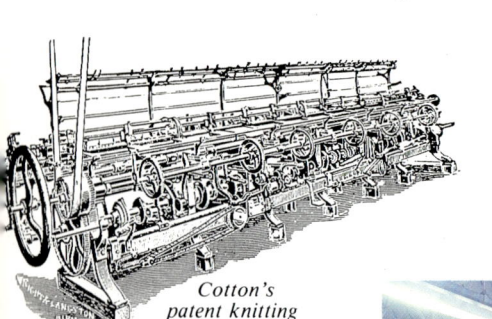

Cotton's patent knitting machine

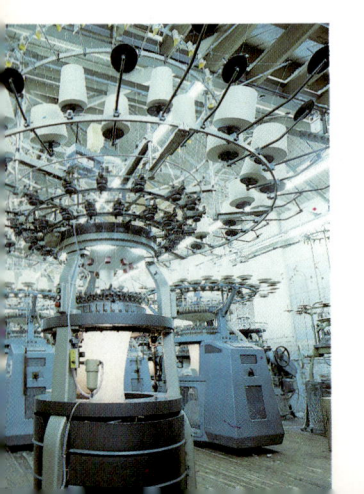

Modern hosiery production at Towles plc

Brush Electrical Engineering Company

'The Brush' has long been Loughborough's largest factory group.

It all started when Henry Hughes owned the Falcon Works on Derby Road in 1855. His factory made saddle-tank locomotives and horse-buses. In 1863, he moved to a site by the Midland Railway Station.

One horse omnibus

Then in 1889 Charles Brush, an American inventor of dynamos, arc-lamps and street lighting, bought the Falcon Works.

Soon Brush produced equipment to supply whole towns with their first ever electricity. At the same time it was constructing 250 tramcars a year.

1892 Brush hydro-generator

Another product was steam locomotives. In 1904 two Parsons turbines were made for Loughborough's first power station in The Rushes. Between 1901 and 1905, cars were produced. The new Great Central Railway ordered Brush rolling stock in 1906. By 1910 there were 2000 Brush employees.

In World War I the first Brush aircraft to be

An early Brush car

constructed was a reconnaissance aircraft, the Maurice Farman S.7 Longhorn, shown below.

Leicester's new bus fleet in 1924 all had bodies built by Brush. The last tramcars were soon followed by the first trolleybuses in 1932, then in 1933 came the horizontal diesel engine. In World War II the Brush war effort turned to aircraft repair and the building of army vehicle bodies, gun mountings and the Dominie aircraft.

Postwar developments included new diesel locomotives, made both for British Rail and for export.

In 1949 bus body production totalled 60 a month, but has since been discontinued. The workforce in 1960 was 4300.

A modern turbo-generator

An artist's impression of the latest Class 60 diesel electric locomotive

Today the Brush (now a subsidiary of the Hawker-Siddeley Group) serves the electrical industry worldwide.

John Taylor & Co – Bellfounders

The Taylor family have been producing bells since 1784 – first at St Neots, then from 1821 at Oxford and from 1839 in Loughborough. The first site here was in Packhorse Lane and the first task was to recast All Saints Church bells. Loughborough was a good central location because the canal system and the new railway could both bring in raw materials and then deliver the new bells.

In 1860 the growing business moved to a larger site – the Cherry Orchard by Freehold Street – and by 1892 Taylors had become the world's largest bellfoundry.

In 1881 John Taylor was engaged to cast 'Great Paul' for St Paul's Cathedral in London. This was the largest bell to be cast by a bellfounder in Britain and weighed over sixteen tons.

Old Foundry engraving

Great Paul *on the way to London*

1887 proved a busy year as many bells were ordered to commemorate Queen Victoria's Jubilee.

Loughborough's carillon, built as a memorial to the dead of the Great War, reflects the importance of bells in the town.

Loughborough carillon is built of local bricks. It contains 47 bells

Bell metal is about 77% copper and 23% tin alloy. The molten metal is poured into a casting mould consisting of an inner core and outer case. The newly cast bell is tuned by removing metal from the interior face on a vertical lathe. Tuning forks and electronic instruments are used in this process

35

Ladybird Books Ltd

In Victorian times Harry Wills owned a bookshop in the Market Place, and also ran a lending library for which borrowers paid a yearly subscription. In 1873 he bought the nearby printing works, called the Angel Press, and published Wills' *Loughborough Almanac, Trade Guide and Street Directory*. This became an annual event for over seventy years. William Hepworth joined the Angel Press in 1906 and the firm then became Wills and Hepworth.

When the earliest Ladybird series appeared in 1915, most of the pictures were in black and white. The firm also continued to print catalogues and advertising material for many national companies, the results growing more attractive as printing technology progressed.

The composing room, Angel Press

H Wills' printing department, 1900

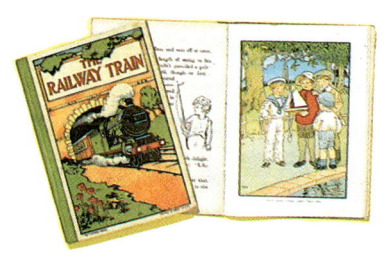

Some of the first Ladybird books

The colourful Ladybird book of today was first produced during the Second World War. Later Ladybird was one of the first to publish information books for children.

Ladybird Books is now one of the most successful international children's book publishers, producing millions of books each year. Sales are worldwide and books have been printed in over sixty different languages.

Full colour printing presses in operation

Davy Morris Ltd – Crane Works

In 1884 Herbert Morris first set up business in London to make pulley-blocks. Later he moved to Sheffield to make cranes and hand-operated lifting equipment. When he started to look for a better site for his factory he chose Loughborough because it was a growing town with a railway, canal, water supply and electrical power.

Canal-side Empress Works

So in 1887 he built the Empress Works (East Works) by the canal near Moor Lane. Later, in the new West Works he installed his own power station! By 1903 Morris was making cranes to lift up to fifty tons; many were exported. By the time of the Great War of 1914-18, he had to build the South Works – to boost production.

The North Works was built next to the Midland Railway in the 1920s to make overhead travelling cranes and steam cranes, and dockside cranes began to appear in many of the world's largest ports.

Motor salvage crane of the 1920s

When the 'container' revolution started in the 1960s, British Rail were amongst the first to order container cranes for all their freightliner terminals.

Today, the modernised Davy Morris Ltd continues to export worldwide, concentrating its efforts in four main areas: heavy cranes (up to 250 tons), hoists, industrial cranes and warehouse automation.

A container crane in Hong Kong

Chemical and Scientific Industries in Loughborough

A number of major scientific and chemical firms are based in Loughborough.

Fisons Pharmaceuticals is an international health care business with its headquarters in Derby Road. The firm has discovered many medicines for the treatment of allergies such as asthma, hayfever, food and eye diseases. It also has highly sophisticated facilities for the research and development of both new and improved medicines based in Loughborough.

Fisons originated in 1921 in the Genatosan Company in Loughborough, which manufactured Sanatogen nerve tonic. The name Sanatogen is now even more widely known through a range of vitamins

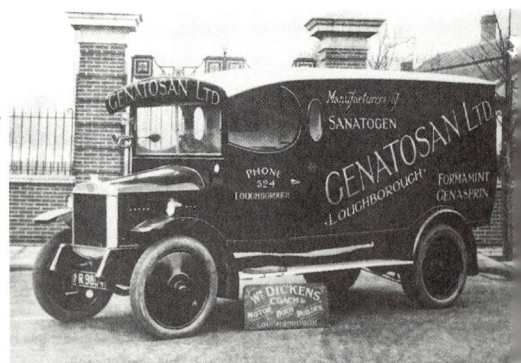

When there was a shortage of laboratory glassware during the Second World War, Fisons supported Colin Clegg, a Loughborough glassblower, to fill this gap.

In the course of time the Loughborough Glass Company became Fisons Scientific Apparatus Ltd, part of the Fisons Scientific Equipment group

3M Health Care Ltd has well over six hundred health care and pharmaceutical products. The firm's health care products are used in the fields of infection control, assessment and therapy, patient care, vision care, orthopaedics and dentistry, while their pharmaceutical preparations are mainly for treatments related to the heart and lungs, and the relief of pain.

Stahl Chemicals (GB) Ltd is in business to produce chemical finishes for the leather, shoes and plastics industries, while plastic shapes such as ducting (tubing) for electrical and telephone cables, as well as vacuum-formed plastics, are made by B & H (Leicester) Ltd.

A typical vacuum-formed shape made by B & H (Leicester) Ltd for a shop-window display

41

Education and Schofield

Herbert Schofield led the Technical College from simply serving the town to meeting national needs. His idea of training on production was first used in 1915 to enable Belgian refugees in local factories to make shells for the army.

Herbert Schofield

By the end of the Second World War the College had grown so large that in 1950 it was divided into five parts. These were the College School (now Burleigh College), the College of Art, the Technical College, the Training

The University campus from the air

College and the College of Technology. In 1966 the last became the University, and in 1977 the Training College, later renamed the College of Education, became part of the University. The idea of a university had been suggested in 1888, with the grammar school as its focus – the grammar school has since become one of the main public schools in Britain.

Loughborough is known all over the world for the education of engineers, of librarians, of physical education specialists, and for its wide ranging research and teaching of many forms of technology. Its physics department has pioneered the use of holograms. Some of its leading engineers have invented and developed the 'Locstitch' machine for textiles.

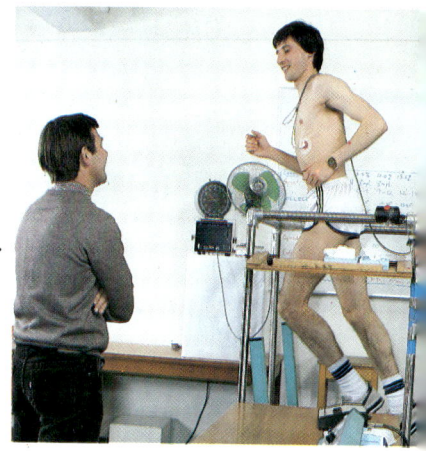

Its students have included many record-breaking athletes, Sebastian Coe among them

'Locstitch' machine

Some Charities

The oldest charity in Loughborough was started to maintain the bridge over the river Soar at Cotes. Money left over from this was used to support a school which became known as the Thomas Burton Charity.

Later some of the money was spent on repairs to the old Church Gate School, the building of a new Boys' Grammar School (1852) and a new Girls' High School (1879).

A royal visit for Dr Barnardo's in Market Street in 1985

John Hickling left property – in 1677 – to pay for poor boys to be taught a trade. In 1683 Bartholomew Hickling left land to pay for a school for twenty poor girls, who were also to be given books, dresses, shoes and stockings each year. In 1713 John Storer gave property to pay for gifts of food for the poor of Loughborough, and for six or eight 'plain coats' to be provided each year to poor children between the ages of five and twelve.